Mr. No-Shoulders

Written by

Jimmy Ewing

Illustrated by

Anne Zimanski

First Printing, 2019

ISBN: 978-1-7923-1923-5

For Dad, the originator of Mr. No-Shoulders:
outdoorsman, father, mentor, teacher, and friend.

Mr. No-Shoulders lives next to me,
But not in a house,

An apartment,

Or tree.

He's under the porch,

On the steps,

By the road.

He makes his living
On mice, rats, and toads.

You better look out!
And know your colors and shapes,
Because Mr. No-Shoulders lives wherever you traipse.

Keep reading, dear friend, and take a look at the map,
to learn where these snakes live, quick as a snap.

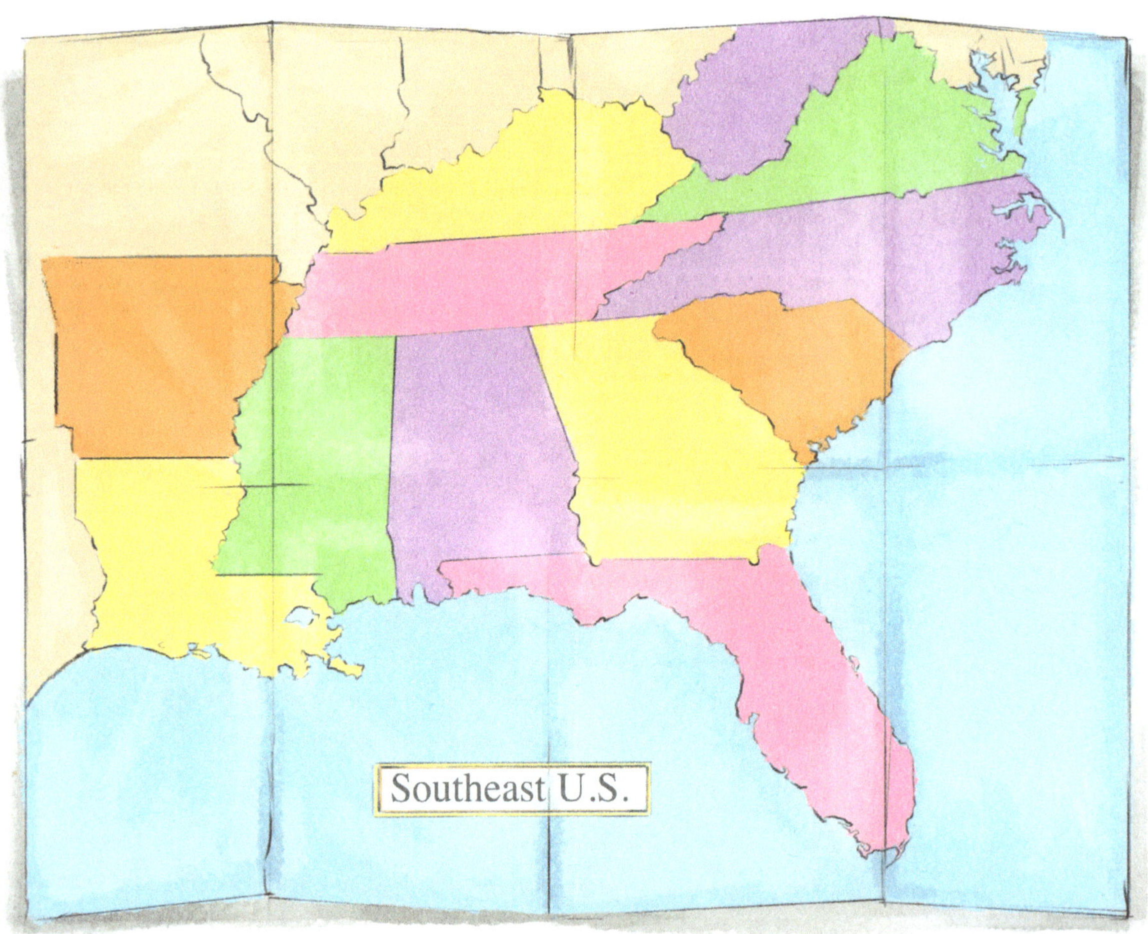

Mr. Diamondback rattler buzzes fast, dry, and raspy.
His big bite can hurt, it can burn, and get nasty.

His rattling sound is unique to his breed,
If you're not ven-o-mous it is nothing you need.

So remember to listen and keep one ear out,
For that dry buzzing sound – near your ankles, no doubt.

When we see Mr. Diamondback what do we do?
Holler "Dad!", back away, and make sure others do too.

Mr. Copperhead snake comes in all sorts of sizes,
So you better look sharp when that wedge-shaped head rises.

He lives in the leaves, but loves warm roads at night.
If you live in the city, your garage is just right!

The big ones have fangs that are huge,
Hooked and long!
Even small copperheads' venom is ever so strong!

Before they grow large their tails can be yellow,
But don't think they're cute! They'll still kill a fellow.

When we see Mr. Copperhead what do we do?
Holler "Dad!", back away, and make sure others do too.

Mr. Cottonmouth Moccasin never backs from a fight.
He earned that strange name with a mouth bright and white.

His keeled scales are dull and he's short, thick, and fat.
If I were a swamp creature, I'd take note of that.

He lives in the wetlands and swamps roundabout.
He looks like a log with a body so stout.

When we see Mr. Cottonmouth what do we do?
Holler "Dad!", back away, and make sure others do too.

Now Mr. Coral Snake is something quite new.
He's colorful, yes, but so deadly too.

His colors in order: red, yellow, black,
Warn all other creatures to stop and stay back!

He is shy like a hermit and hunts mostly at night.
Lizards and frogs are his greatest delight.

His cobra venom, to me, seems somewhat extreme,
Since he carries enough to kill a whole team!

Like so many creatures – he has a near double,
But Mr. Scarlet Kingsnake causes no trouble!

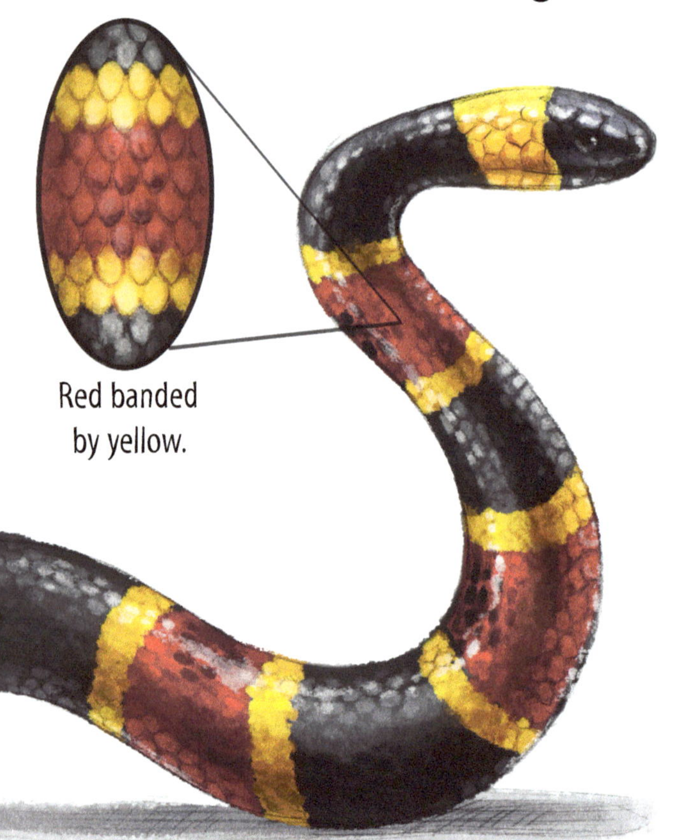

Red banded
by yellow.

Eastern Coral Snake
Micrurus fulvius
Venomous

Red banded
by black.

Scarlet Kingsnake
Lampropeltis elapsoides
Nonvenomous

When we see Mr. Coral Snake what do we do?
Holler "Dad!", back away, and make sure others do too.

Mr. Pygmy Rattlesnake is really quite small,
and he carries less venom than the rest of them all.

But the small birds and lizards that make up his prey,
don't notice the difference and they don't get away!

He's so very small you may not hear his warning.
"Don't tread on me," he says. "Not this morning!"

When we see Mr. Pygmy Rattlesnake what do we do?
Holler "Dad!", back away, and make sure others do too.

Last, but not least, Mr. Canebrake – the end.
His pretty black stripes show he's nobody's friend.

We gave him two names – "Timber Rattler" the other.
And he likes to hang out in the thickest of cover.

Under tin,

piles of wood,

Sticks,

stones and debris,

Sometimes he will even climb up in a tree!

When we see Mr. Canebrake what do we do?
Holler "Dad!", back away, and make sure others do too.

There are so many snakes that live near your door,
And knowing about them helps even the score.

In the Southeast U.S., these are the ones you should fear.
The rest are all harmless – I hope it's now clear.

But you don't have to worry – they don't want to play,
And biting small people isn't part of their day.

All the same, please be smart and alert when you're out,
And listen to me so you'll know what to shout!

Eastern Diamondback Rattlesnake
Crotalus adamanteus

Copperhead
Agkistrodon contortrix

Water Moccasin (Cottonmouth)
Agkistrodon piscivorus

Eastern Coral Snake
Micrurus fulvius

Timber Rattlesnake (Canebrake)
Crotalus horridus

Pygmy Rattlesnake
Sistrurus miliarius

When we see Mr. No-Shoulders what do we do? ...

Holler

And make sure others do too!

Gray Rat Snake
Pantherophis spiloides
nonvenomous